I LOVE TO GO TO DAYCARE
AMO ANDARE ALL'ASILO

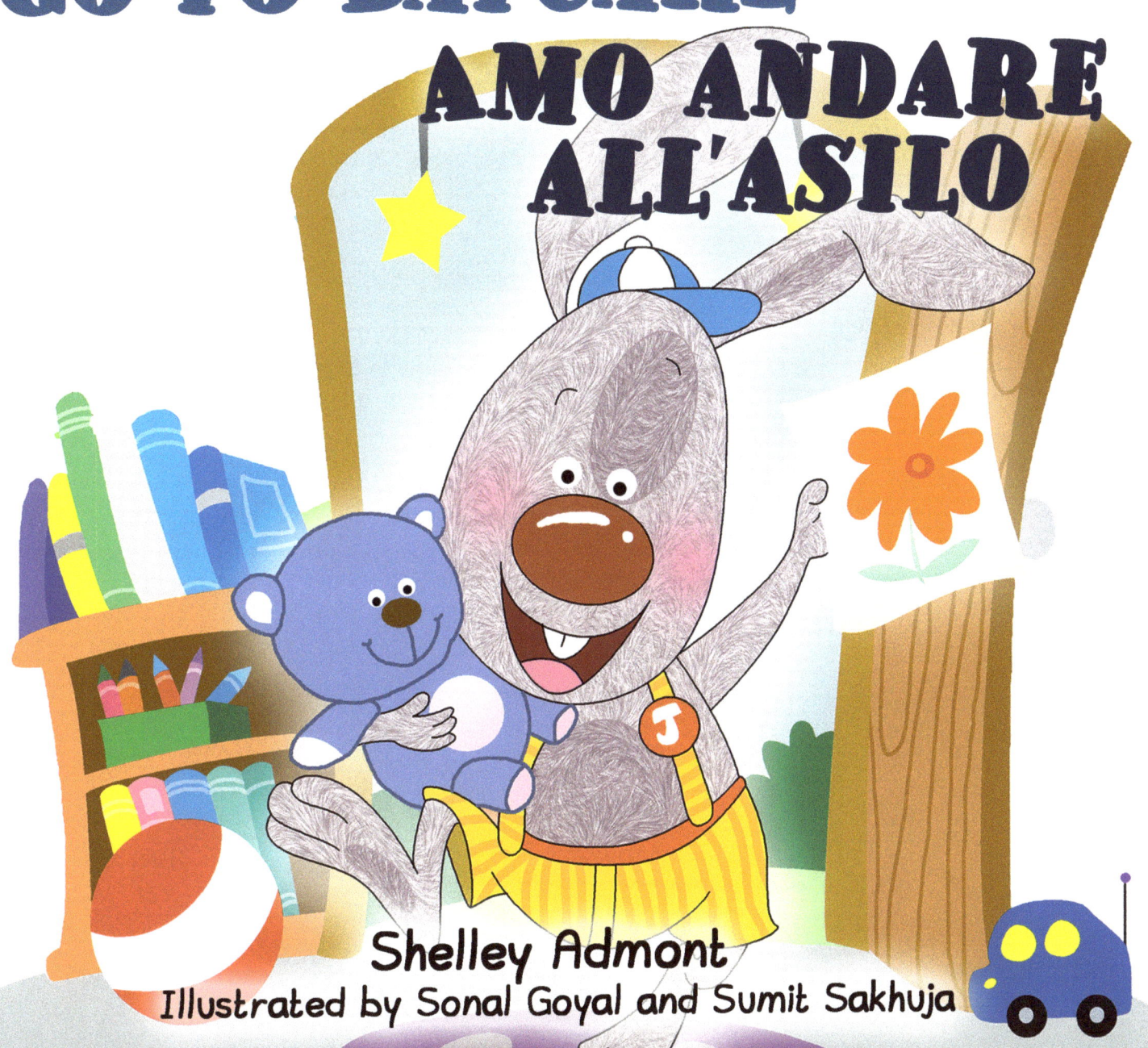

Shelley Admont
Illustrated by Sonal Goyal and Sumit Sakhuja

www.kidkiddos.com
Copyright©2014 by S.A.Publishing ©2017 by KidKiddos Books Ltd.
support@kidkiddos.com

All rights reserved. No part of this book may be reproduced in any form or by any electronic or mechanical means, including information storage and retrieval systems, without written permission from the publisher or author, except in the case of a reviewer, who may quote brief passages embodied in critical articles or in a review.
Second edition

Translated from English by Annalisa Langone
Traduzione dall'inglese a cura di Annalisa Langone

Library and Archives Canada Cataloguing in Publication
I Love to Go to Daycare (Italian Bilingual Edition)/ Shelley Admont
ISBN: 978-1-5259-3342-4 paperback
ISBN: 978-1-77268-509-1 hardcover
ISBN: 978-1-77268-104-8 eBook

Please note that the Italian and English versions of the story have been written to be as close as possible. However, in some cases they differ in order to accommodate nuances and fluidity of each language.

For those I love the most-S.A.
Per quelli che amo di più-S.A.

Jimmy was lying in his bed hugging his favorite teddy bear. He was really trying to sleep, but something bothered him and kept him wide awake.

Jimmy era seduto sul suo letto mentre abbracciava il suo orsacchiotto preferito. Stava cercando di dormire, ma c'era qualcosa che lo preoccupava e lo teneva sveglio.

He rolled out of bed and went to look for his parents.

Si alzò e andò a cercare i suoi genitori.

Down in the living room, his mom and dad were watching TV. Holding his teddy, Jimmy sat on Mom's lap. "Mommy, I can't sleep," he said.

Giù in salotto, la mamma e il papà stavano guardando la TV. Tenendo in mano il suo orsacchiotto, Jimmy si sedette sulle ginocchia della mamma e disse: "Mamma, non riesco a dormire".

Mom ruffled his hair and gave him a kiss. "What are you thinking about?"

La mamma gli scompigliò i capelli e gli diede un bacio. "A che cosa stai pensando?"

"I'm thinking about daycare," he whispered and hugged Mom tightly.

"Sto pensando all'asilo", sussurrò e abbracciò forte la mamma.

"Oh, sweetie, daycare is so fun!" said Mom.

"Oh, tesoro, l'asilo è così divertente!", disse la mamma.

"You'll meet new friends there," added Dad. "In fact, it's so much fun that I wish I could go, too!"

"Lì incontrerai tanti nuovi amici", aggiunse il papà. "È così divertente che andrei anch'io!"

"Can I stay at home with you?" asked Jimmy. His head fell on Mom's shoulder.

"Posso rimanere a casa con te?", chiese Jimmy. Appoggiò la testa sulla spalla della mamma.

Mom stroked his head, looking deeply into his eyes. "How about this," she said. "Since it's your first day in daycare, you'll only stay there for two hours. After that, I'll come back to take you home. But I'm sure that you'll have so much fun that you won't even want to leave."

La mamma gli accarezzò la testa, lo guardò intensamente negli occhi e disse: "Cosa ne pensi di questo, dato che è il tuo primo giorno d'asilo, rimarrai lì solo due ore. Poi ti verrò a prendere e torneremo a casa. Ma sono sicura che ti divertirai così tanto che non vorrai andar via."

"You know what?" said Dad. "You can even take your teddy bear with you. Does that sound good?" Jimmy nodded.

"Vuoi sapere una cosa?", disse il papà. "Puoi portare con te anche il tuo orsacchiotto. Cosa ne pensi, campione?", Jimmy annuì.

"Oh, you're such a big and smart boy," said Mom, kissing his forehead. "I'm sure you're tired. Let's go to bed."

"Oh, sei così grande e intelligente", disse la mamma dandogli un bacio sulla fronte. "Sicuramente sei stanco. Andiamo a dormire".

She led Jimmy to his room and tucked him in. Then, she gave him a goodnight kiss and whispered in his ear, "I love you, sweetie."

Portò Jimmy nella sua cameretta e gli rimboccò le coperte. Gli diede il bacio della buonanotte e nell'orecchio gli sussurrò: "Ti voglio bene, tesoro".

"I love you too, Mom," said Jimmy. With a big yawn, he hugged his teddy bear and closed his eyes.

"Ti voglio bene anch'io, mamma", disse Jimmy. Sbadigliando, abbracciò il suo orsacchiotto e chiuse gli occhi.

Jimmy was almost asleep when he heard a strange voice. "Hey, Jimmy!"

Jimmy si era quasi addormentato quando udì una strana voce: "Ehi, Jimmy!"

He opened his eyes, looking around. "Who's talking?" murmured Jimmy.

Aprì gli occhi, si guardò intorno e mormorò: "Chi è che parla?".

"It's me, your teddy bear!"

"Sono io, il tuo orsacchiotto!"

Astonished, Jimmy looked down. The teddy bear waved his hand and smiled. "I saw you were upset," said the teddy bear.

Jimmy stupito guardò verso il basso. L'orsacchiotto mosse la sua mano e sorrise. "Ho notato che sei turbato", disse l'orsacchiotto.

Jimmy sighed deeply. "Yes, I'm going to daycare tomorrow," he mumbled.
Jimmy sospirò profondamente e mormorò: "Sì, domani andrò all'asilo".

"Jimmy, my friend, but I'm going with you!" The teddy bear winked at Jimmy and gave him his big teddy-bear smile. "I'll watch you there, and we'll have a great time together."
"Jimmy, io verrò con te!" L'orsacchiotto gli fece l'occhiolino e un gran bel sorriso. "Io sarò lì a guardarti e ci divertiremo molto insieme".

Jimmy looked at him jumping and clapping and burst out laughing.
Jimmy lo guardò saltando e battendo le mani e scoppiò a ridere.

"Shhhh," whispered the teddy bear. He pointed to Jimmy's two older brothers, who were sleeping in their beds.
"Shhhh," sussurrò l'orsacchiotto. Indicò i due fratelli più grandi di Jimmy mentre dormivano nei loro letti.

He jumped into Jimmy's arms and cuddled him close. "Goodnight, my friend!"

Saltò tra le braccia di Jimmy e lo abbracciò. "Buonanotte, amico mio!"

The next morning his two older brothers jumped out of bed and walked over to Jimmy.

La mattina successiva i due fratelli più grandi saltarono giù dal letto e andarono verso Jimmy.

"Today is your first day in daycare. You are so lucky," said his oldest brother.

"Oggi è il tuo primo giorno di asilo. Sei così fortunato", disse il fratello maggiore.

Jimmy was excited but a little bit worried. "I'm only going for two hours today," he murmured. "Is it a long time?"

Jimmy era emozionato ma anche un po' preoccupato. "Oggi andrò solo per due ore", sussurrò. "È troppo tempo?"

"Not really," said the oldest brother.
"You won't even stay for a nap," added the middle brother.

*"Non proprio", disse il fratello maggiore.
"Perché non rimanere anche per un pisolino", aggiunse il fratello più grande.*

During breakfast Jimmy was very quiet. "Are you ready to go, Jimmy?" Mom asked, after he cleared his plate.

Durante la colazione Jimmy era molto tranquillo. "Sei pronto per andare, Jimmy?", chiese la mamma, dopo aver tolto il suo piatto.

"I guess," he answered looking down at his teddy bear. The teddy bear gave him a big smile and Jimmy felt much better.

"Credo di sì", rispose guardando in basso verso il suo orsacchiotto, il quale gli fece un bel sorriso e Jimmy si sentì molto meglio.

He took his teddy bear in one hand and Mommy's hand in the other and they set out.

Prese il suo orsacchiotto in una mano e la mamma nell'altra e si avviarono.

"You'll like it, honey," said Mom while they were walking. "And I'll be back in two hours, right after snack time."

"Ti piacerà, tesoro", disse la mamma mentre camminavano. "Torno tra due ore, subito dopo l'ora della merenda".

"I know, Mommy. I'm fine. I have my teddy bear with me." Jimmy winked at his bear.

"Lo so mamma. Sono tranquillo. Ho il mio orsacchiotto con me", Jimmy fece l'occhiolino al suo orsacchiotto.

"I'm so proud of you, my big boy," said Mom as the pair walked up to the daycare's door.

"Sono così orgogliosa di te, ragazzo mio", disse la mamma avvicinandosi verso la porta dell'asilo.

Mom knocked twice, and a lady appeared at the door.
La mamma bussò due volte e arrivò alla porta una signora.

"Hello, Jimmy," the lady said. "We have been waiting for you. Come on in!"
"Ciao, Jimmy", disse la signora. "Ti stavamo aspettando. Entra!"

"How does she know me?" Jimmy whispered to his mom.
"Come fa a conoscermi?", Jimmy sussurrò alla sua mamma.

Mom smiled. "I called her before and told her we were coming."
La mamma sorrise. "L'ho chiamata prima e le ho detto che stavamo arrivando."

There were a lot of other kids there. Some of them were playing with cars, and others were playing with dolls.
C'erano tanti coniglietti. Alcuni di loro stavano giocando con le macchinine e altri giocavano con le bambole.

"Let's go have some fun. Come on, Jimmy!" the teddy bear said. Smiling, Jimmy turned to Mom.

"Andiamo a divertirci. Vieni, Jimmy!", disse l'orsacchiotto. Sorridendo, Jimmy si girò verso la mamma.

"Go have fun, sweetie," she said. "I'll pick you up right after snack time."

"Vai a divertirti, tesoro", disse. "Verrò a prenderti subito dopo l'ora della merenda".

"I remember. Bye, Mom!" Jimmy yelled as he ran to play with a large truck.

"Mi ricordo. Ciao, mamma!" Jimmy urlò correndo a giocare con un grande camion.

After two hours, Mom came back to the daycare to pick up Jimmy. He ran to meet her and gave her a huge hug.

Dopo due ore, la mamma tornò all'asilo per prendere Jimmy. Le corse incontro e le diede un grande abbraccio.

"Mom, it was so much fun!" he shouted. "I played with a large truck, and then I painted a flower for you all by myself!"

"Mamma, è stato così divertente!", urlò. "Ho giocato con un camion grande e poi ho dipinto un fiore per te, tutto da solo!"

Mom smiled happily. "It's so beautiful. What else did you do today?"

La mamma sorrise felice. "È bellissimo. Cos'altro hai fatto oggi?"

"The teacher read us a book, and after that we ate a snack," Jimmy said in one breath, bouncing near Mom.

"La maestra ci ha letto un libro e poi abbiamo fatto merenda. Era così appetitosa", disse Jimmy d'un fiato, rimbalzando vicino alla mamma.

"Can I stay for longer tomorrow? Please, Mom!"

"Posso rimanere di più domani? Ti prego, mamma!"

The next day, he stayed longer. The day after that he stayed even longer.
Il giorno successivo, rimase più a lungo. Il giorno dopo, ancora di più.

Now, Jimmy spends the whole day in daycare having lots of fun! He loves to play games and paint, to hear stories and eat.
Ora, Jimmy rimane tutto il giorno all'asilo a divertirsi! Ama giocare e dipingere, ascoltare storie e mangiare.

He is also happy when naptime comes, so he can rest a little bit.
È felice anche quando arriva l'ora del pisolino, così può riposare un po'.

Sometimes Jimmy doesn't bring teddy bear with him,
A volte Jimmy non porta con sé il suo orsacchiotto,

but when he comes back home from daycare,
Jimmy tells him all about his day.
*ma quando torna
a casa dall'asilo,
gli racconta tutto
della sua giornata.*

www.ingramcontent.com/pod-product-compliance
Lightning Source LLC
LaVergne TN
LVHW072010060526
838200LV00010B/324